MW01602051

Very Young Catholics
in India

Emily Koczela

Written by Emily Koczela

© 2025 Emily Koczela

Published by Holy Heroes LLC

PO Box 12, Cramerton, NC 28032
United States of America
1-855-Try2B-Holy (1-855-879-2246)
www.HolyHeroes.com

ISBN 978-1-959418-07-8

Other books in this series

Very Young Catholics in Togo

Very Young Catholics in Austria

Very Young Catholics in Taiwan

Very Young Catholics in Fiji

Very Young Catholics in Ireland

Very Young Catholics in Canada

Very Young Catholics in Kenya

Very Young Catholics in Ecuador

Very Young Catholics in the United States

Very Young Catholics in Iceland

Very Young Catholics in Argentina

Very Young Catholics in Australia

Very Young Catholics in Thailand

Very Young Catholics in Brazil

Very Young Catholics in Dubai

Very Young Catholics in New Zealand

This book is one of a series of books about very young Catholics around the world. The stories and locations in this book are true to life, but the specific details are drawn from many children's lives. We have changed names and details to protect the privacy of the families and the children. Thank you to the real children and parents who served as our sources and our photo models.

Contents

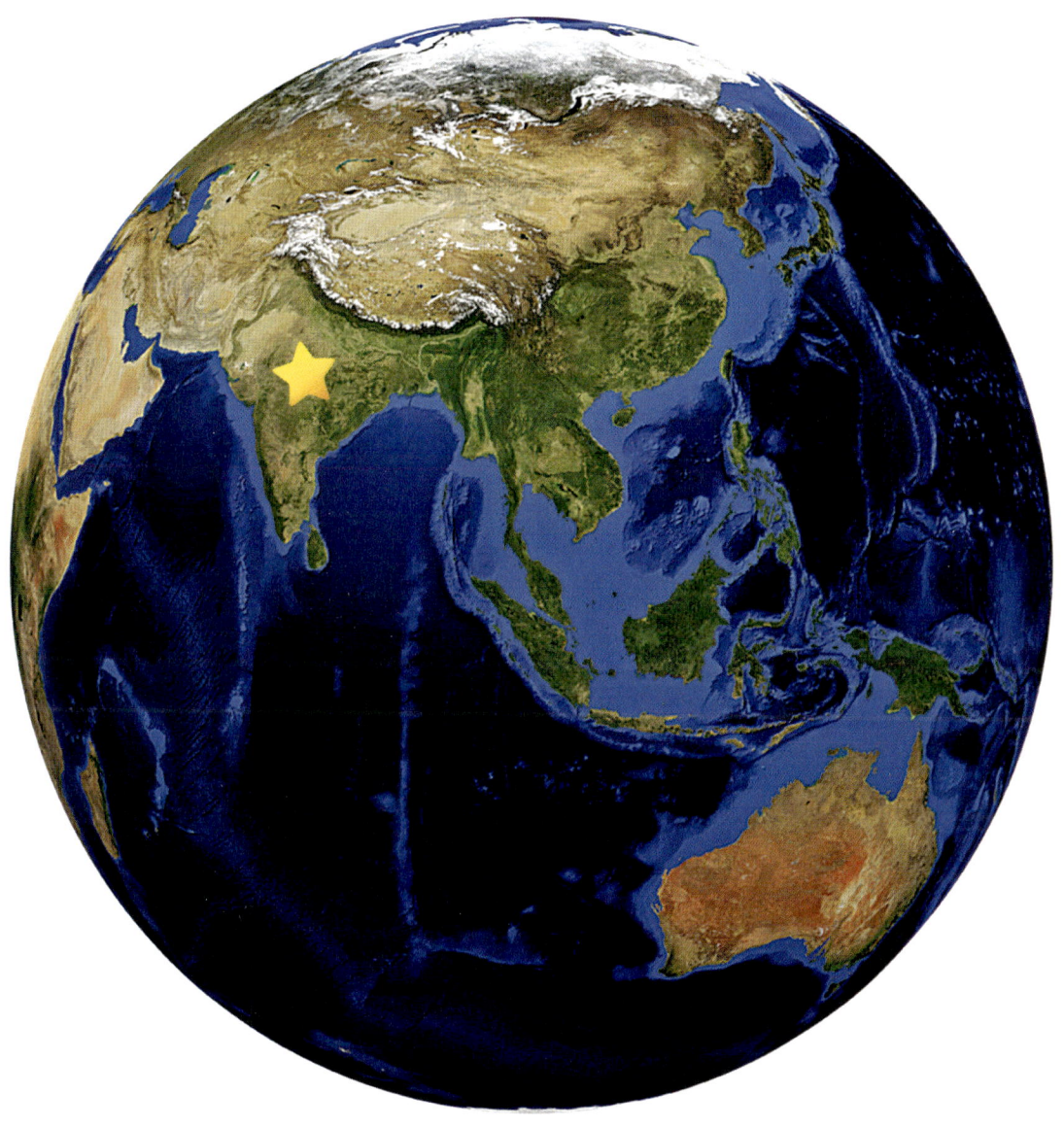

Here is a picture of the earth from space.

The gold star shows the location of India, at the far south of the Asian continent.

Prologue

A friendly family lives on a busy street in a big city in India. Each of the children has two names. The first name is for a great saint of India, and it is in the English language. The second name is a word that lifts our hearts to God, and it is in the Hindi language.

Thomas Pratham is eleven. His first name honors the Apostle Thomas, who came to India after Jesus' resurrection. Pratham means first, recalling that God is the First and the Last.

Nathan Pragyan is nine. His first name honors the Apostle Nathaniel, who also came to India. (We don't always realize that we are hearing about Nathaniel because he is sometimes called Bartholomew.) Pragyan means wisdom.

Alsa Prerna is seven. Her first name is a shortened version of Alphonsa and honors the first canonized saint who was born in India, while her second name means inspiration.

Mariam Prarthana is two. Her first name honors Saint Mariam Thresia, a visionary Indian nun who was canonized in 2019. Prarthana means prayer.

There are twenty-two major languages in India, so children in India have lots of words for father and mother, but this family says Da and Ma.

Chapter I
Picnic on the Terrace

The children live in a warm and sunny part of India. That means that they can be outside as much as they are inside. The terrace outside their home is the setting for everything from hanging laundry to having fun. The best fun came when Ma and Da started a custom of a Thursday night picnic dinner of thanksgiving on the terrace.

4

The first step of the picnic is to go shopping for food at the market. Their city has giant gleaming stores full of food, but Ma and Da like to buy their vegetables at the local outdoor market where the same families have been selling vegetables to Da's family for several generations. The market is near enough that all the children, except for Mariam, can walk there. But Mariam wants to go, so Da gives all the children a ride to the market on the motorcycle. You can only see Mariam's legs in the picture because she is hiding her face. She really doesn't like having her picture taken!

5

"What are we buying today?" asked Thomas.

"Cauliflower," Da said.

"Cucumbers," Nathan added.

"Beans," Mariam squeaked.

"Tomatoes, peas, squash, potatoes, onions," Alsa rattled off. "And herbs and hot peppers. And we are going to visit all our friends at the market while we are buying things."

6

The market stalls were piled high with brilliant colors. Da and the children filled their bags with vegetables from many different sellers, stopping to chat with each of them. One of their friends at the market gave each of them a carrot to munch as they finished shopping.

"Do we have enough?" asked Alsa, looking at all the bags of fresh vegetables and herbs.

"We have so much my arms are weighted down," said Thomas. "Three full bags of vegetables? That should keep us all busy eating for a week!"

Early in the evening, as darkness began to fall, Ma stirred up some delicious vegetable dishes. Da lit the barbecue fire while Alsa sprinkled spices on the chicken. Thomas and Nathan strung colored lights overhead.

Soon everything began to smell so good that it was hard to wait for dinner.

"We could play ball while we wait," said Nathan.

"There's just one problem," said Thomas. "We might kick the ball right off the terrace. It could land on someone's head down in the street."

They hung over the side and inspected everyone passing below.

"There aren't too many people right now," said Nathan. "We probably wouldn't hit anyone. But maybe we would. That would be big trouble."

"They never look up and see us," Alsa said, "but maybe they smell our delicious dinner and wonder who is cooking."

"Let's tell jokes," said Thomas. "Then they will hear us laughing too."

"I have one," said Nathan. "I can jump higher than the Taj Mahal."

"No, you can't," said Alsa. "No way."

"Yes I can," said Nathan. "The Taj Mahal can't jump!" Alsa giggled.

"I have one," said Thomas. "Why did Da think that Alsa was a tomato when we were going around the market today?"

Da looked over from the barbecue fire. "Why did I what?" he asked.

"Well," said Thomas, "you kept telling her to ketchup," and he chuckled proudly as everyone else figured out his meaning and began laughing.

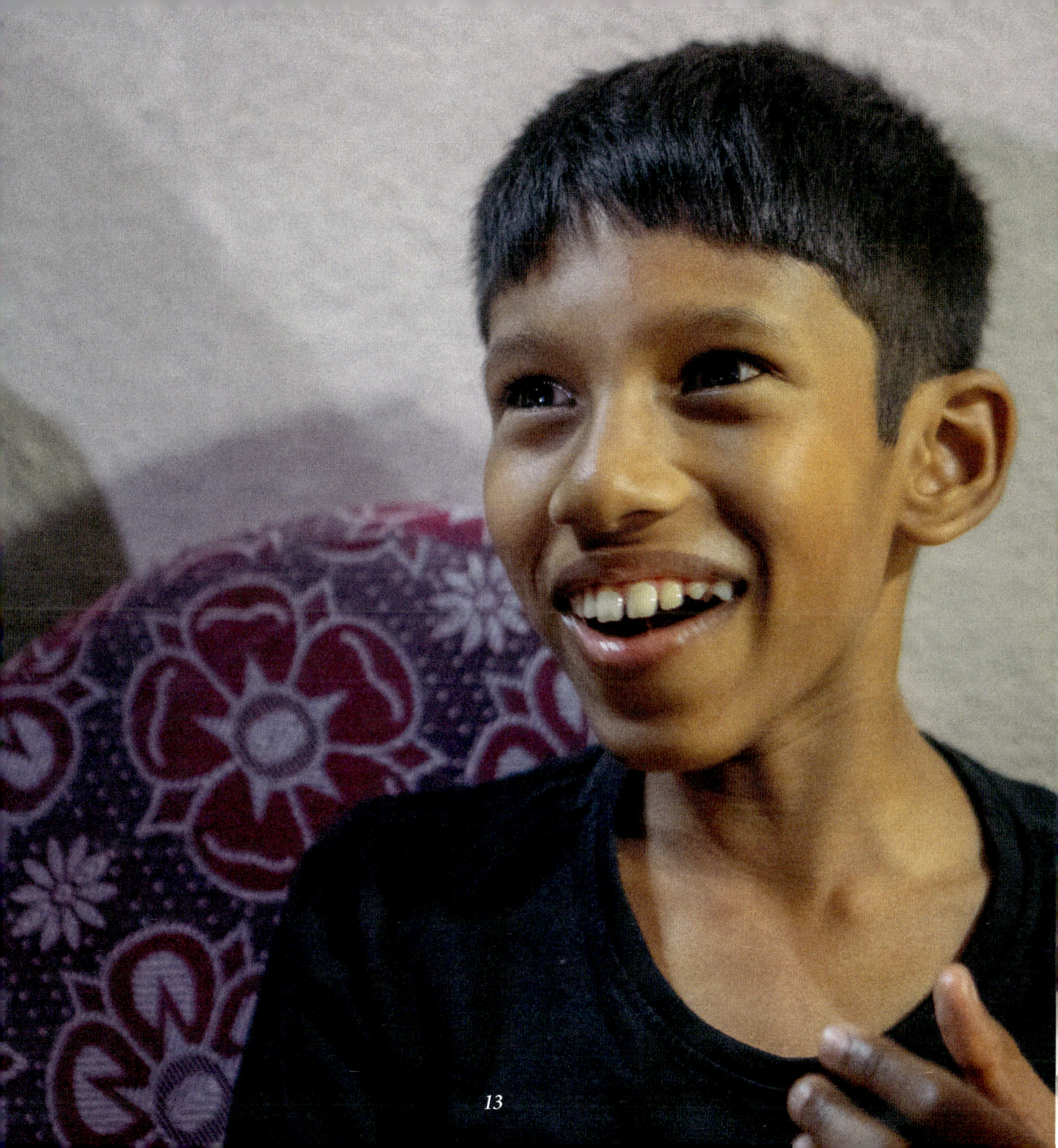

Finally, Da said that the food was ready. They sat down around the picnic cloth and began their thanksgiving prayer. They thanked God for the gift of His love and the love of each other. They thanked Him for all the delicious food and asked for a blessing on everyone who helped to grow it or cook it. Then they all filled their plates with chicken, vegetables, and a flat bread called chapati.

14

"We are just like the birds," Alsa said gleefully. "We are perched up high between the street and the sunset."

It was a blessed time.

Chapter II
Dinosaurs

On weekdays, Ma and Da get up at 4:00 in the morning while it is still dark and cool. Then they take turns; each day one of them goes to Mass while the other one prepares breakfast and lunch for the older children. All three must be fed, in their school uniforms, carrying their lunch, and out the door to the school bus by 7:20 in the morning. Da goes to work at the same time, so it is quite a busy start to the day.

16

The children go to Catholic schools, and like children all over India, they have a lot of school work. They also have difficult examinations every year in science, math, social studies, and two different languages.

The weekend after the examinations, the children said wistfully, "We would like to do something that does not involve answering any questions. We have answered every question on the examinations and our brains have nothing left in them."

"I know just the thing," said Da. "Some terrible monsters will stop you from thinking about the examinations."

The room fell silent as all the children stared at him, wondering if he was going to produce a terrible monster out of his pocket. Da had a mischievous expression on his face and his eyes were twinkling.

"We will go visit some terrible monsters, but they will be at the museum, so they will just be carvings," he said.

Nathan was delighted. He loved going to the museum. He thought the scorpion carving was hilarious and every time they went to the museum, he would lie on its back and pretend it was going to give him a ride somewhere.

On the other hand, Mariam was not sure what a museum was or what a carving was, but she was sure she didn't want to visit any monsters.

As soon as they got to the museum, she caught sight of the gigantic figure of a *Tyrannosaurus rex* with huge teeth.

"I knew it," she sniffled quietly to herself. "Nobody has any sense around here except me, and I am only two years old. Doesn't anyone else notice that we are visiting a dangerous monster?"

"You don't have to be scared," Thomas said kindly, noticing her expression. "This dinosaur is not real. He is carved out of plaster. The real creatures lived millions of years ago, so they cannot hurt you. And maybe they were really nice. Nobody really knows because there weren't any people on earth when the dinosaurs were alive, so nobody wrote down anything about them. Maybe the *Tyrannosaurus rex* was just in a bad mood because he wanted ice cream, and he couldn't find any because it hadn't been invented yet." This absurd tale made Mariam feel better, even though it made everyone else laugh.

"I like the *Tyrannosaurus rex*. In fact, I like every dinosaur," said Nathan. "And I might even study dinosaurs when I grow up. Explorers found lots of dinosaur fossils up in northern India in Gujarat, but there are thousands of places in India where no one has checked for dinosaur fossils yet. Maybe I will discover some unknown type of Indian dinosaur."

"Like what kind of dinosaur?" said Alsa.

"Well, I don't know until I find it," said Nathan, reasonably.

Titanosaurus

"Should we just call it the *Idontknowasaurus*?" asked Thomas.

"Ha-ha, very funny," said Nathan. "I already know about the gigantic Indian dinosaur called the *Titanosaurus*. I have also heard of Indian dinosaurs called *Isisaurus* and *Jaklapallisaurus*. Those are cool names. People who discover new dinosaurs get to name them, so I might name mine the *Nathanasaurus*. That would make me very famous."

Isisaurus

"You know dinosaurs are ugly, right?" said Alsa.

"I don't care," said Nathan. "I am not putting the *Nathanasaurus* in a beauty contest."

"If you find one that isn't ugly, you could name it after me," Alsa offered cheerfully.

"Well," Nathan said, "there was a type of dinosaur called an *oviraptor* that had a tail that could fan out like a peacock. Scientists can tell by the fossils of its bone structure. Everybody thinks peacocks are beautiful, and the peacock is the national bird of India. No one has found an *oviraptor* in India yet, but maybe I will find a beautiful peacock *oviraptor* in India and I can name it after you."

Jaklapallisaurus

22

He thought for a while, and then added, "But maybe I will do that after I find a very cool ferocious dinosaur to name after myself."

Oviraptor

23

Chapter III
Visiting the Stone Elephant

"Da," asked Thomas one day, "what is the biggest creature in India? All the dinosaurs are gone from the earth. So what is the biggest creature that is left?"

"The biggest creature in India now is the elephant," said Da. "Most of them live far away in the wild, but we could go see a stone elephant if you want to. It is as big as a regular elephant."

"Let's go see it, let's go see it!" chanted Alsa.

"Let's go, let's go!" echoed little Mariam.

The stone elephant stands in the middle of a great flat sandy area, strewn with rocks of all sizes. All around the elephant are small buildings (called *rathas*), each one carved out of a single enormous stone.

"What do you think of the stone elephant?" Ma asked.

"I like him," said Alsa. "Or maybe it's a her. I hope she is not too hot standing there in the sun all day."

"She is granite," laughed Thomas. "Sun, wind, monsoon rains, even a tsunami, she doesn't care. She has been here for more than a thousand years already, and she may be here a thousand more."

25

"Now we must travel around all of the rathas without once touching the ground," proposed Nathan. "Come with me!" He set off clambering over the rocks.

"We can pretend that the ground is all deep water, and we must leap from rock to rock," said Thomas, springing along like an energetic tiger.

"Don't fall in the water, don't fall in the water!" squealed Alsa as she scrambled across the dry rocks.

"Yes, it is full of crocodiles!" whooped her brothers, as they leaped from boulder to boulder.

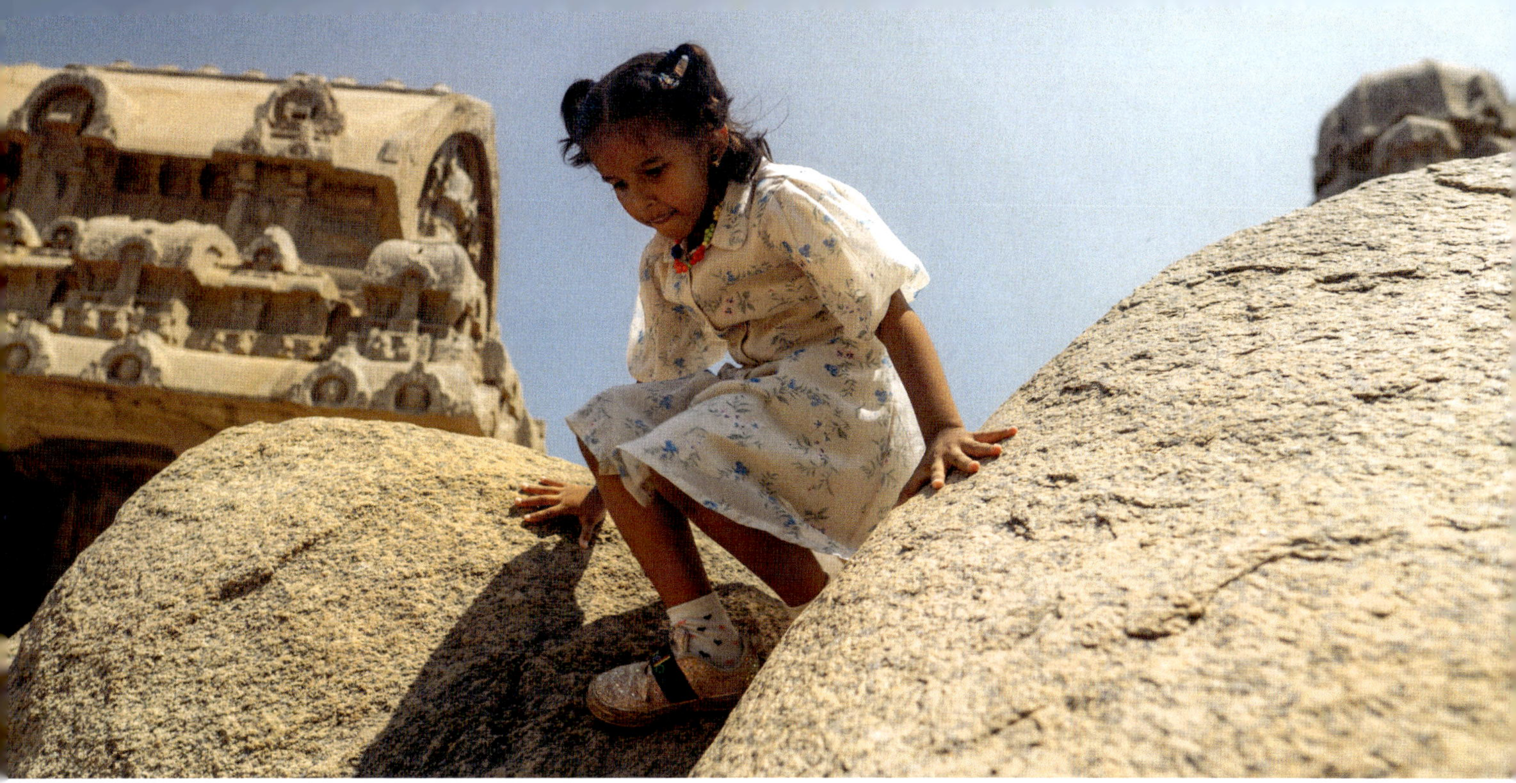

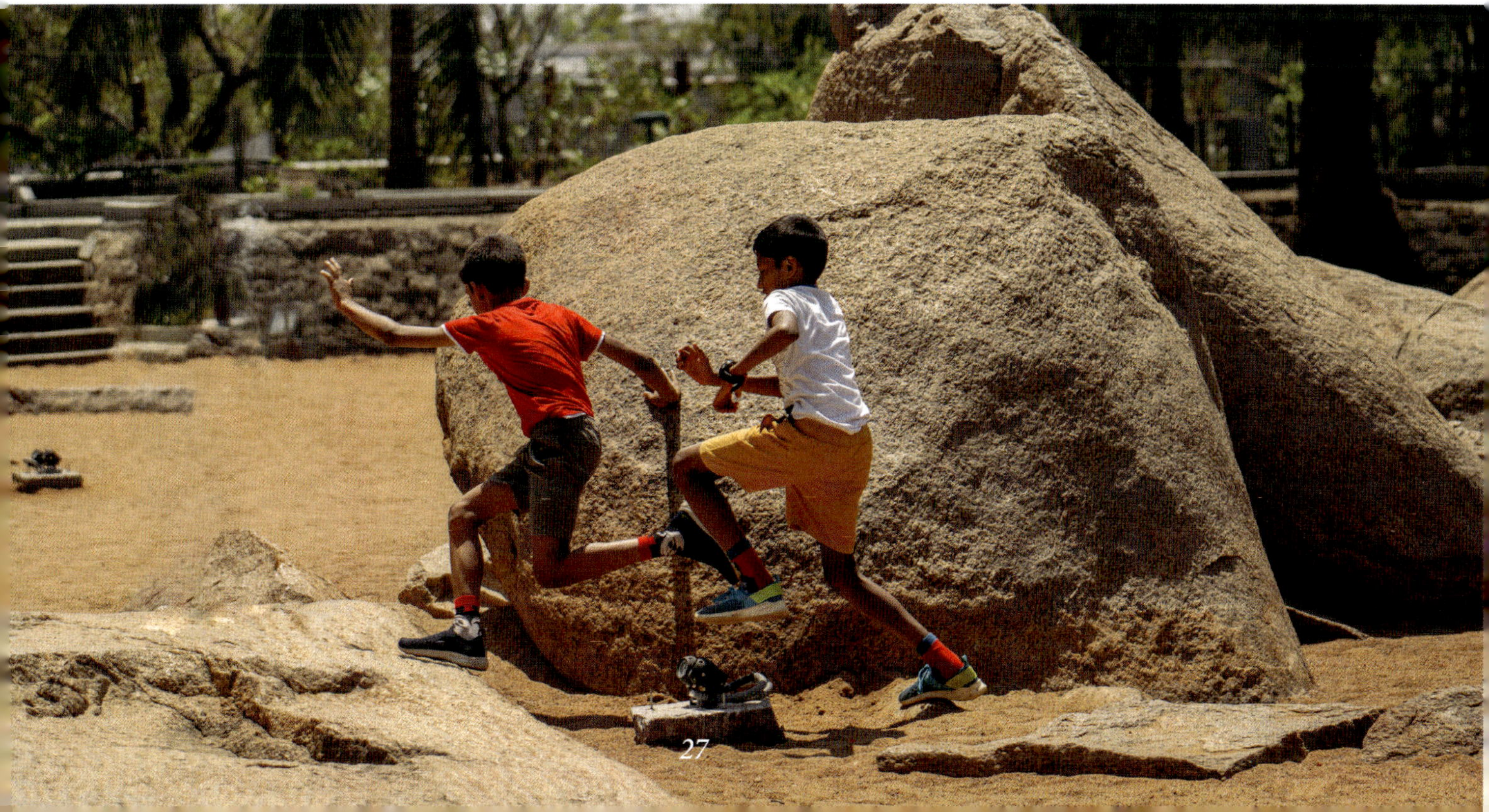

When they were quite hot and tired, they came back to Ma and Da and Mariam on the shady side of a ratha.

"I think I can push these pillars until this ratha falls down," said Alsa, pushing until she was out of breath.

"Somehow, I am not too worried," said Thomas. "The only person who pushed a building down that way was Samson in the Bible, and I really don't think you are as strong as Samson."

"There is a crack in the roof, but I think it was there before we got here," said Nathan.

"Are you all ready to see some more things?" asked Da. "We can go find something to cool us off, and on the way, we will see a huge wall that is all covered with carvings, including more elephants. We can finish up at the hill with the giant stone ball."

The children beamed. "That's a great idea! We can get watermelon and pineapple to cool off," they said. "We have been running very hard."

Refreshed with some juicy fresh fruit, they clambered up a steep hill where a gigantic boulder sits. The boulder looks as though it might roll down any second, but it is actually quite stable. Visitors over the centuries have tried to push it down the hill, but it never budges.

The hill where it sits is covered with a slippery, chalky powder, so it is fun to slide down. All the children took turns. Even little Mariam tried it.

The only thing that made them stop was when Da spoke those wonderful words, "It's time to have lunch."

What a great idea! They could sit down. They could wash their hot faces and hands. They could have a tray with crunchy appalam, and ten different spicy sauces to put on rice. To cool off their mouths, there was a sweet milky pudding flavored with cardamom. And at the end, there were candied fennel seeds to chew.

Yum!

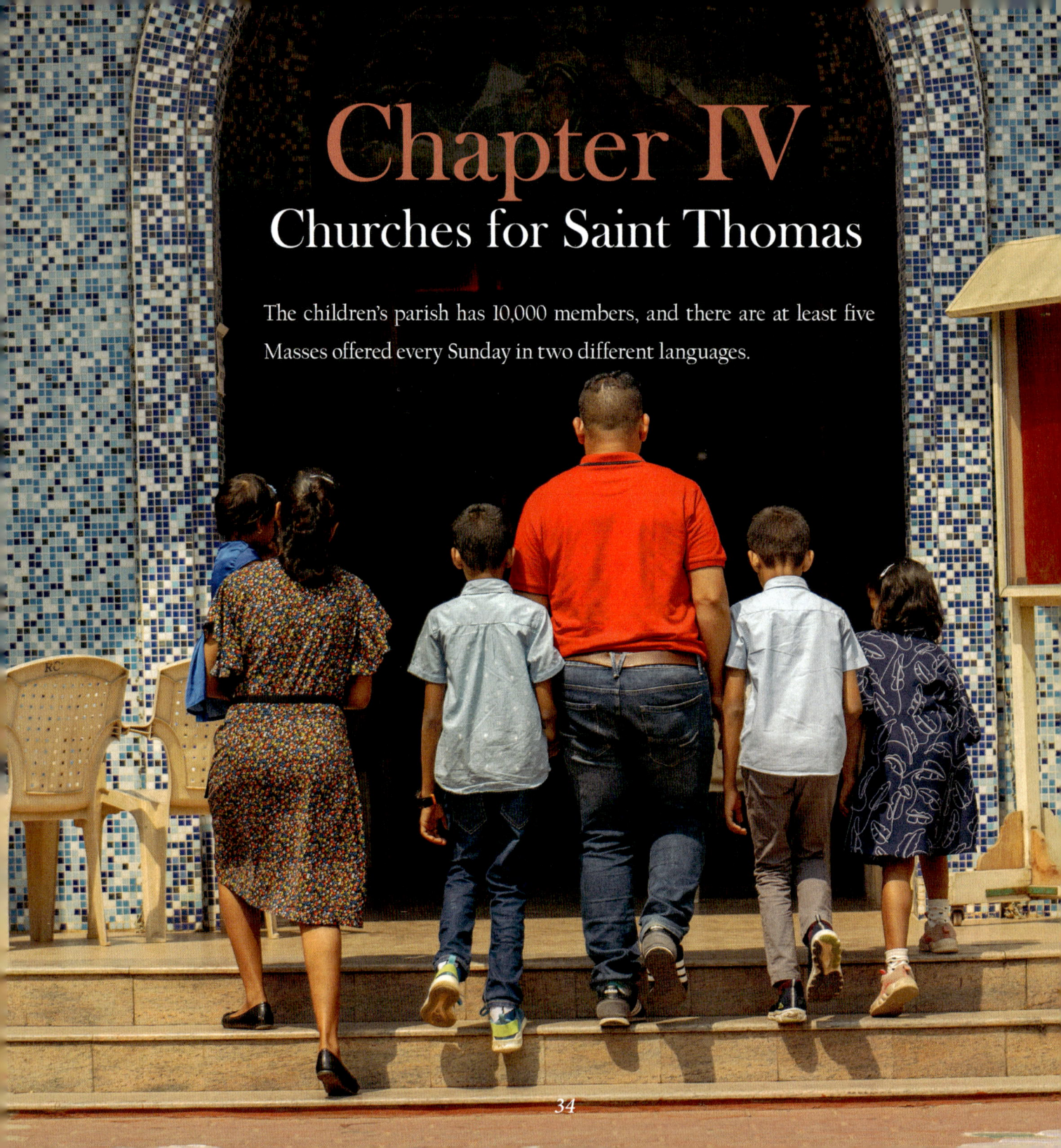

Chapter IV
Churches for Saint Thomas

The children's parish has 10,000 members, and there are at least five Masses offered every Sunday in two different languages.

After Mass, Ma and Da often take the children to their favorite beach. India has thousands of miles of coastline and lots of beautiful beaches. People come to play games along the sand, enjoy the fresh breeze, and create giant sand constructions.

"Saint Thomas the Apostle came to this coast," said Da. "We named you for him, Thomas. He preached and baptized beside the sea a little further north."

"I've always liked Saint Thomas because he came all that way from Jerusalem to India," said Thomas. "That was really brave. Maybe I will make him a church out of sand."

"I'll help," said Nathan. "Where should we put it?"

"I'll mark a big circle with my feet right where it should go," said Thomas.

35

"I'll start piling up walls," said Nathan.

"I know Saint Thomas already has a beautiful cathedral in the city," Thomas said. "But he was from a small town on the Sea of Galilee. He probably played on the beaches there when he was a little boy. Maybe he will like our little sand church."

"He has another church near here," said Nathan. "Remember the one where you start at a big archway at the bottom of 160 steps and then walk up the steps to get to the church? We walked up all of them on a very hot day. And there are lots more churches named for Saint Thomas over in western India, where he came first."

"Well, this sand church will not last as long as those beautiful buildings," Alsa said. "But maybe it will make Saint Thomas smile in Heaven because we are still thanking him after all these years."

"It will be here for a little while at least, before the tide comes in," Thomas said, looking out over the water.

"Can you imagine being one of the people who first heard him talking about belief in a loving God who created this beautiful earth?" Thomas went on. "And he brought the good news of forgiveness of sins and eternal life."

41

"If someone came and told me that there was one God and He loved me, and I could be free of my sins and live forever, and then that person invited me to be baptized, I would jump right in the water as fast as I could," Nathan exclaimed, jumping to his feet and leaping forward to show exactly how fast he would move.

They all stood for a moment, looking out to sea and thinking of Saint Thomas.

Then Ma noticed their long shadows. "It is getting towards sunset," she said. "It is time to go home."

42

43

They turned and started making their way back to the car.

"We brought some watermelon to eat before we get in the car, so you won't be hungry or thirsty on the way home," said Da, "and we have a jug of clean water to wash off all the sand and watermelon juice after that. You don't want to ride home all scratchy and sticky."

"We can sing songs and play games in the car," Alsa suggested eagerly. "Ma, can you teach us some new songs?"

"Of course," said Ma. "I know lots more songs to teach you. Funny songs, story songs, and even a lullaby or two in case Mariam starts to fall asleep!"

They strolled along through the gathering golden light of sunset. And far away, on a hill overlooking the city, near the church of Saint Thomas the Apostle, the statue of Saint Thomas with Jesus glowed in the golden sunset light.

45

Chapter V
Train Trip

Railroads are popular in India. Tracks run all across the country, and millions of people travel by rail every day. The railroads have been functioning a long time. Some of the train cars are so old that the railroad company has taken them off the tracks and hauled them away to a playground. The children love to climb on them.

"We are all going on a trip," the children called, leaning out of a passenger car and waving. "Goodbye, goodbye."

"Where are you going?" Ma called back.

"We are going to visit the Taj Mahal," Alsa said.

"And then we are going to the dinosaur museum in Gujarat," Nathan added.

"And then we are going up to the Himalayas to see real snow," Thomas finished.

"Let's sit in the freight car now," said Alsa. "Let's pretend it is full of gifts and toys and books and games, and we are going to travel around India giving some to every kid that we see."

"If that train were moving, the conductor would make you pull your legs inside and go sit in your seat," Ma laughed. "So I am afraid this is an idea that will never come to pass."

"True," said Alsa with a grin. "Also, I do not have a freight car full of toys and games. But it is fun to pretend."

"I like this train playground," said Thomas, "but I like it even better when we go on real train trips."

48

"Like the trip we take every year to go on pilgrimage to the great cathedral at Velankanni," Nathan exclaimed. "And we are going again next week, aren't we, Ma?"

"Yes," Ma responded. "Da and I are getting everything ready. Da has purchased our tickets on the overnight train. We will sleep on the train and arrive in the morning before the sun is up."

"Hurray!" the children rejoiced. "The sleeper car is fun."

On the day of the trip, the children went to school all day, came home, and put on comfortable clothes for the overnight train. Crowds of people filled the station, but the family followed closely behind Da until they came to their sleeper car.

50

There were berths on each side of the compartment and berths on the corridor section, so there was room for all the family to be close to each other. Soon everyone was spread around comfortably. Alsa was on one top berth, Nathan was on another, and Thomas was on the third. Ma, Da, and Mariam were lower down.

"I will ask some train riddles while we are waiting to start," Thomas offered cheerfully. "If an electric train is going south, which way does the smoke go?"

Everyone looked quite blank until Nathan said, "This is a crazy question. An electric train does not have any smoke."

"Right!" said Thomas.

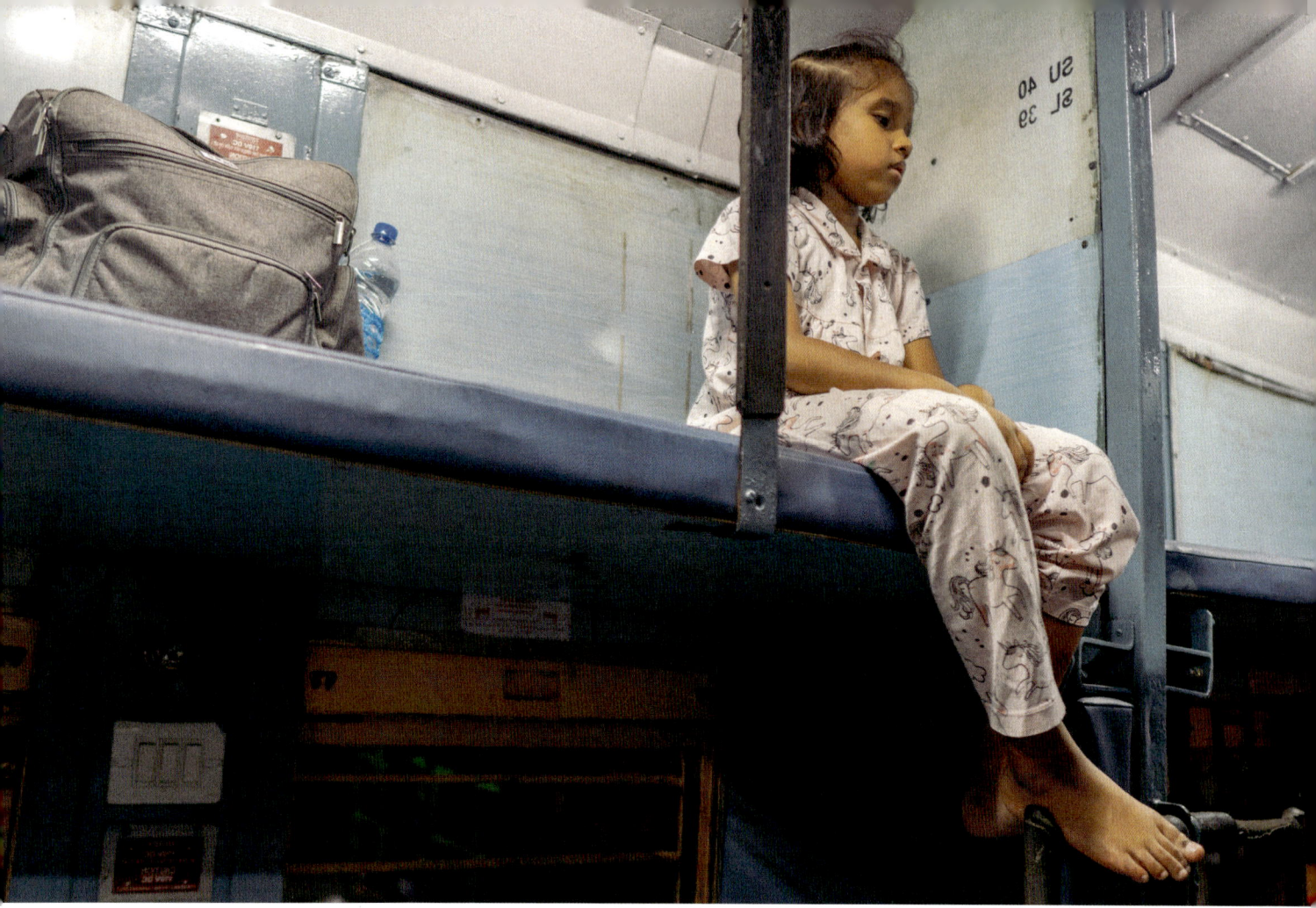

Just then the train began moving. "The only sad thing is that now we are going to ride hundreds of miles across India, and we will not see anything because it will all be at night," sighed Alsa.

"When we went to see your grandparents last year, we were wide awake on the train for an entire day," said Ma. "You have already seen thousands of colorful sights of India from the trains. Now it is time to say your night prayers and go to sleep."

53

Nathan and Thomas grinned, rolled over, and were soon asleep. Alsa was still restless, though.

"Ma," she whispered, hanging over the side of her berth. "I can't sleep."

"Shhh," Ma said quietly. "Lie still and the train will rock you to sleep." She stood up and brushed Alsa's hair off her forehead with a gentle hand.

"Someday you will ride a train up to the magnificent snowy mountains in the north of India," she began softly. "And another time you will ride a train down to the very tip of southern India and watch the sun rise on one side of you and set on the other." She spoke even more softly as she saw Alsa's eyes begin to close. "And other times your train will pass tea plantations and ancient ruined palaces and huge wildlife sanctuaries with tigers and elephants, and it will travel over long bridges and through tunnels and past waterfalls and beautiful blue lakes." Ma's voice was so soft now that it was only a gentle whisper. "And you will pass so close to the villages that the field flowers will brush the train, and you will see the children playing kabaddi and smell the dinner that their mother is cooking, and when you are tired of traveling, you will come home to Da and me." Her quiet voice faded away as Alsa's deep breathing showed she was asleep. Ma slipped back to her own berth, and soon she was asleep too.

55

Chapter VI
On Pilgrimage

Hours later, Da woke everyone. They quickly put on their shoes and grabbed their backpacks. The train only stops for three minutes at Velankanni, so they had to be ready. Fortunately, pilgrims who arrive in the dark like this can go to the pilgrim hostel to sleep until the sun rises and they can see the great cathedral.

When it was time to start the day, Da gathered everyone together. "Let's talk about being on pilgrimage," he said. "You step out of your ordinary life. You walk away from the things you usually think about. You walk in a sacred place. You turn your thoughts towards God. You try to make your heart big enough to welcome Him and quiet enough to hear what He is saying to you.

"People can walk for years on pilgrimage to a holy place. Or they may go for one day, like us. The important thing is to take time from your life to be sure that your heart and your will are in union with God."

"We are ready!" said the older children.

"But what about Mariam?" asked Alsa. "She is too little to understand."

"She will learn by watching us," said Da. "If we pray, she will try to pray too. And Jesus knows exactly what to expect of pilgrims who are only two years old. They cannot pray like an adult, but their innocence gives them a special place in His heart."

Then the family went out into the bright shiny morning with the thousands of other pilgrims who were visiting that day.

61

They began with Mass. The main basilica at Velankanni is dedicated to Our Lady of Good Health, and people come from all over India to pray for healing. They ask Mother Mary's intercession for all their needs. A great saint of India, Mother Teresa of Calcutta, used to say a prayer that everyone else can say too: "Mary, Mother of Jesus, be a mother to me now."

There is a beautiful outdoor path lined with the Stations of the Cross, and, after Mass, the family prayed their way from one end to the other.

The sun was high in the sky and it was very hot, but the Stations of the Cross bring to mind the worst hours of Jesus's life and death, and He did not complain, so they also did not complain.

After praying the Stations, the family went around to all the other beautiful chapels at Velankanni. In one chapel, they approached the altar on their knees.

Imagine if you suddenly saw a vision of God in all His majesty. You would not just stand there. You might fall to your knees, or you might even fall flat on your face. That is why, in this holy place, the children went to the altar on their knees. Even Mariam!

65

"Da," said Thomas, "what happens if people come to Velankanni to ask the one God for something, even though they do not believe in Him?"

"God loves all people," Da responded. "He can see into every heart, and He knows why each person comes here. Those who pray to Him in faith as their loving Father will receive His grace and help on all that is wrong and sorrowful in their lives. Those who treat God as a magic machine for giving them what they want will find nothing. They will not ask God for all He is willing to give, and they will not accept what He offers."

"And what does Mother Mary do?" asked Thomas. "All these chapels have her name on them."

"Mother Mary always does one thing," said Da. "She points people to her Son. People ask her to pray with them and for them, and she says the same thing she said on earth. 'Do whatever my Son tells you.'"

"I remember when she said that!" said Nathan. "At the wedding in Cana."

"And every day, one way or another, she says it again," said Da.

66

When night fell, the family prepared to leave. "We have spent the day with God," Ma said. "We have brought all of our life before Him and asked Him what His will for us is. We have prayed for blessings for everyone who is in need. Now we must pick up our ordinary lives again."

The children picked up their things.

They waited for the train peacefully, and rode home through the night.

But pilgrims who come home are never just the same as when they left. They have stopped to remember that our entire earthly life is a pilgrimage toward Heaven. That makes each day precious and important.

Chapter VII
Advent and Christmas

"Speaking of journeys," Ma said one evening, "our next journey is the Advent journey toward Christmas."

"The Christmas story has everything," said Da. "Stars, angels, singing, shepherds, visiting strangers, a beautiful mother, a gallant protector, and a sweet baby."

"We have four weeks to get ready," Ma said. "It is the fourth Sunday before Christmas, and the first day of Advent."

"I will take care of the Advent wreath," said Nathan.

"It looks nice," Ma said. "I think everyone can have a turn lighting a candle one week, except Mariam. She is too young."

"I can put together the stable for the Nativity scene," Thomas offered. "I remember how to do it from last year."

"I can find the figures for Mary and Joseph and the baby and all the animals that live in the field," Alsa added cheerfully. "I will also put in all the rocks that we painted with our prayers to the baby Jesus."

Thomas took the family's potted plants from the terrace and placed them all around the stable, creating a field of wheat, fenugreek, and ragi. Since the plants were alive, they kept growing all through Advent, so Thomas had to keeping cutting the field with a pair of scissors.

In another corner, the family set up a table-top Christmas tree. Live evergreen trees rarely grow in a warm climate like the one where the children live, but Ma and Da had found a copy of a small one for their Christmas celebration.

Mariam was amazed. Like tiny children all over the world, she could not believe that her parents were bringing a tree inside the house! But also like children all over the world, she thought it was a great idea. She kept asking, "Tree? Tree?" and then giggling, as though perhaps the family had not noticed that there was suddenly a tree in their house.

73

Even though there was telling of Christmas stories, lighting of Advent candles, praying, cooking, and preparing for Christmas guests, time moved along slowly through Advent. Finally, a beautiful, warm and sunny Christmas Day arrived.

"I will light all the candles, including the white Christmas candle!" Alsa said.

"I know lots of Christmas songs about Jesus and Mary and the angels and the shepherds, and I am going to sing them all day," Thomas said.

"I am going to help cook a giant dinner," said Nathan.

There was a great bustle getting ready for Christmas Mass. There they prayed and sang and rejoiced. Then they came home and cooked a feast of all their favorite foods.

Finally, they tried to take a Christmas picture of the children.

75

Unfortunately, as you know, Mariam hates to smile for pictures.

But in the end, she did. It was a happy Christmas.

The children will keep playing and praying as they grow up in their beautiful city. Their parents and their whole parish will watch over them and help them grow. Each Sunday, they will go to Mass and join in prayer with all the other children who are also going to Mass all over the world. They will be part of the faithful prayer of the Mass that has been going on for hundreds of years. They will pray for their brothers and sisters in Christ all over the world. That includes you! Maybe someday you will come to visit.

THE END

Some Things You Encountered in This Book

Location

India is the seventh largest country in the world. It stretches about 2,000 miles from the Himalayan mountain range on the north border to the far southern tip of the mainland, where the cape known as Kanyakumari juts into the Indian Ocean.

It has cold snowy mountains, hot dry plains, huge forests, famous rivers, and miles of ocean coast. It also has the second largest population in the world, at about 1.4 billion people. About 20 million of them are Catholic.

India has been settled for thousands of years, although for most of that time, the region that we now call India was not one nation. Instead, there was a mixture of great empires, small kingdoms, and open tribal regions. There are still remnants of the great empires all over India.

Weather

India is so vast that every kind of weather occurs somewhere. In the far north, among the magnificent mountains of the Himalayan chain, the weather is quite cool, and it snows in the winter. However, most of the country remains warm all the time. In the hottest places, the temperature can get as high as 50 degrees Celsius (or 122 degrees Fahrenheit).

Seasons are defined by the amount of rain. Monsoon season, or the season of heavy rain, can bring as much as 80 percent of the total yearly rainfall in a three-month period. Although the rain is welcome, people have to be careful. Even the ordinary streets can flood in an intense storm.

Taj Mahal

The Taj Mahal is located in the city of Agra, India. It is one of the most famous sights in the entire world. A wealthy ruler had it built in honor of his beautiful wife. Construction began in the year 1632. It took more than twenty years to build and decorate the Taj and then create all the associated buildings and gardens. It is so beautiful that millions of visitors come to see it, including the family in this book!

Saree

The most famous garment of India is the *saree*, which is partly a skirt and partly a sash across the shoulder. Millions of women wear sarees every day, ranging from the cotton sarees worn for ordinary work to the stunning embroidered silk sarees worn for weddings and festivities. The best thing about sarees is that they look nice on every woman.

Little girls do not wear the saree, but they begin early to learn from their mothers how to create the intricate folds and drape the saree over the shoulder. Here you can see little Alsa checking to see how she is going to look when she can wear her own saree.

In the meantime, she can help her mother dress in a beautiful saree for a special occasion. Ma is also adorned with the fragrant strings of jasmine that are traditionally worn in the hair for a big event.

Kabbadi

The most popular sport in India is cricket, but there is another popular sport which is quite unusual. The game is called *kabaddi,* and it is an ancient village game from India which is now played as a professional sport in many countries. Most of its rules are familiar features of other games—a field, a center line, two teams, and an attempt by a player from one team to cross the center line and tag a member of the other team. The distinction in kabaddi is that the player crossing the center line can only stay on the opposing team's side for the duration of one breath and must prove that he or she has not taken a new breath by saying *kabaddi kabaddi kabaddi* over and over the entire time until crossing back onto the original side. This guarantees a fast moving game. Since it requires no equipment, it can easily be played anywhere. That means it is still a village game today.

Saint Teresa of Calcutta

India has a rich tradition of saints. Some came to India from other places, some were born in India and went out elsewhere as missionaries, and some lived their whole lives in India. The most famous Indian saint of recent times was a nun known as Mother Teresa, who worked in the city of Calcutta. She taught school for nineteen years, and then she heard God's call to serve the poorest of the poor. She left the school and began taking care of those living on the streets of Calcutta. Other women joined her, and they created a new order of religious sisters who took a vow to give wholehearted free service to the poorest of the poor. They continue to serve around the world.

"God speaks in the silence of the heart, and we listen.

"And then we speak to God from the fullness of our heart, and God listens.

"And this listening and this speaking is what prayer is meant to be."

—Mother Teresa

89

Travel the world with the

The *Very Young Catholics* series presents a vivid picture of the universal Church through the eyes of children from around the world! Beautifully photographed, these books depict the everyday life of a Catholic family interwoven with Catholic culture, traditions, and doctrine. Collect them all and learn about Catholic families in every time zone!

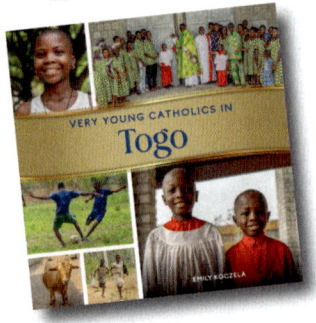

Discover more Very Young Catholics Books and Resources at HolyHeroes.com/VYC

VERY YOUNG CATHOLIC.

Very Young Catholic Project!

Author Emily Koczela is on a mission to visit all twenty-four time zones, discovering the joy of local Catholic traditions and the wonder of God's creation. Jam-packed with gorgeous full-color photos, children will love paging through these astounding books.

The series already includes the United States • Togo • Austria • Taiwan • Fiji • Ireland • Canada • Kenya • Ecuador • India • Iceland • Argentina • Australia • Thailand • Brazil • Dubai • New Zealand *and more on the way!*

HOLY HEROES®

Helping You Bring the Joy of the Faith to Your Family

Put Together the Life of Saint Carlo Acutis

Enjoy making this puzzle collage with photographs from Carlo's life!

Saint Carlo Acutis – "My Life's Plan"

From a very young age, Saint Carlo Acutis was in love with Jesus in the Holy Eucharist. As the first millennial to be canonized, his life is relatable to us today. He enjoyed a lot of the same things we do: skiing, driving a car, owning a pet, and working on the computer. Before his death at the age of fifteen, he built a website for sharing amazing Eucharistic miracles from around the world.*

Featuring real photographs of Saint Carlo Acutis, his family and friends, this big, beautiful puzzle is an enjoyable activity for the whole family (or classroom!). Also be inspired by these words Carlo wrote when only 7 years old (after his 1st Holy Communion): "To be always united to Jesus – this is my life's plan."

672 pieces • 18 x 24-1/2 inches
Unlike most puzzles, ours is NOT made in China!

* You can read about these miracles for yourself at: *https://www.miracolieucaristici.org*

**Find Saint Carlo's puzzle at:
HolyHeroes.com/Carlo**

HOLY HEROES
Helping You Bring the Joy of the Faith to Your Family

Share These Books and Games with your Kids!

Discover the *Dear God* book series

Patti Maguire Armstrong has written a series of books that will captivate young readers with stories they can relate to and learn from. In *Dear God, I Don't Get It*, Aaron Ajax finds his sixth-grade world turned upside down when his family has to move to a new town and away from the comfortable life he's known. He learns about courage and prayer, even when God doesn't seem to listening.

In *Dear God, you Can't Be Serious!*, Luke Ajax is not happy when his parents tell him he will be homeschooled as a fifth grader. Praying hard that he can keep going to school with his friends teaches him that sometimes God answers our prayers in ways that we don't expect.

Each book features engaging discussion questions and is delightfully illustrated by Shannon Wirrenga.

Find the Dear God Series at: *HolyHeroes.com/DearGod*

How Fast Can You *Name-it!*?

Your children will learn the names and meanings of Catholic objects and gestures, awakening in them an appreciation for the wonder of our Catholic Faith. Be warned, Mom and Dad: it's the young ones that can often quickly spy the match—and blurt the NAME out first!

Find this game and many more at:
HolyHeroes.com/Games

HOLY HEROES
Helping You Bring the Joy of the Faith to Your Family

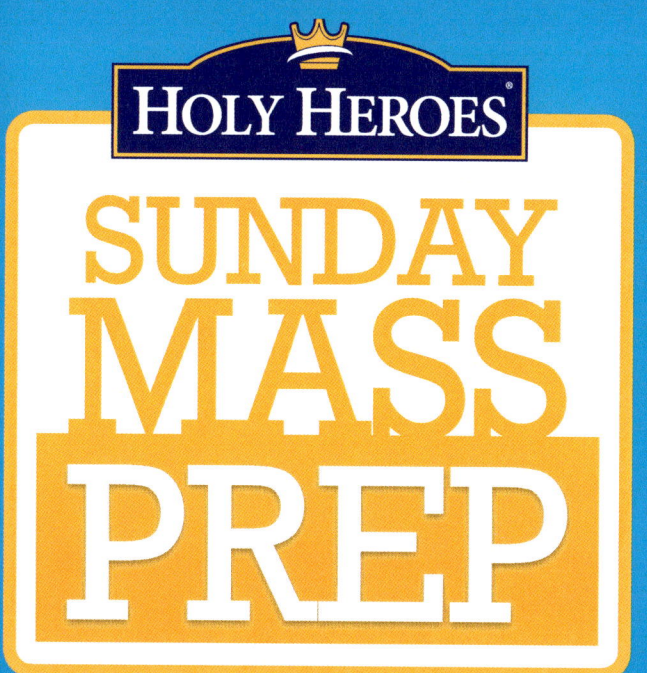

SUNDAY MASS PREP

Sign up for FREE weekly Sunday Gospel Videos and more! Presented BY kids, FOR kids!

Your kids can have fun getting ready for Mass!

Get started at **HolyHeroes.com/MassPrep**

<u>REE</u> weekly materials for Sunday Mass include:

- Gospel videos
- Mass quizzes
- Coloring pages

- Early reader worksheets
- Bonus activities for special feast days

About the Author

Emily Koczela is the Director of the Very Young Catholic project. She is a lifelong Catholic, mother of six, and grandmother of fifteen. Her travels have taken her to Mass in more than two dozen countries. She writes this series to delight and inspire children by introducing them to their brothers and sisters in Christ around the world.

Made in the USA
Middletown, DE
17 November 2025

21456563R00060